# HOUSES OF
# GREAT AMERICANS

*Home Library Publishing Company*
*Fort Atkinson, Wisconsin*

*Henry Wadsworth Longfellow home, Cambridge, Massachusetts.*
*(Courtesy Longfellow House Photo)*

*Frontispiece:* Berkeley, home of Benjamin Harrison,
Charles City County, Virginia. (Walter Miller Photo)

# CONTENTS

# PAUL REVERE HOUSE
## *House of a Silversmith*

Paul Revere lived in Boston, Massachusetts, long before the days of specialization. Still considered one of the nation's greatest silversmiths, he also made eyeglasses and false teeth. Despite this, his greatest claim to fame, as any schoolboy will tell you, was his famous "midnight ride" on the 18th of April, 1775. Henry Wadsworth Longfellow's dramatic version of how "the fate of a nation was riding that night" is long remembered.

His ride, coupled with those of Thomas Dawes and Captain Prescott, aroused the Minutemen throughout every "Middlesex village and farm" to be on guard against the British. It enabled colonial leaders John Adams and John Hancock to move to safety and gave the militia at Concord time to secret their precious supplies — supplies which would come in handy at the upcoming Battle of Bunker Hill.

For many years Revere had lived in a house owned by a Dr. Clark, but in 1770 he purchased the house in the North Square (which is actually a triangle).

As far as is known, during Revere's occupancy it was always a three-story frame dwelling with an ell at the rear, and a medieval-looking overhang at the first level. During the seventeenth century it was a two-story dwelling and it was given its original configuration at the time of its restoration in this century.

In 1908, the Paul Revere Memorial Association purchased and restored the old house, opening it to the public during the same year as a tribute to the true hero of Longfellow's poem.

The Paul Revere House is believed to be the oldest wood-frame house in urban America. (Samuel Chamberlain Photo)

The second-floor study is dominated by a Louis XVI secretary from France. (Creative Photographers Photos)

# ADAMS OLD HOUSE
## A Great Family's Colonial Mansion

Her home in Quincy, Massachusetts, was an oasis to both Abigail Adams and her husband John. As the first lady of the land marooned in a "castle of a house ... the President's House," which she found twice as large as a meeting house, she was pressed for funds to maintain it and obliged to keep thirteen fires daily "or sleep in wet and damp places." No wonder she wrote to her sister, "I long for my rose bush, my clover field, and the retirement of Quincy, and the conversation of my dear sister and friends."

Quincy to Abigail meant a pleasant, isolated, colonial-style house eight miles from Boston with a gabled mansard roof, gray clapboard siding and green shutters. John Adams, who had visited this house with Abigail, bought it while he was overseas serving as United States Minister to Great Britain from a descendant of its original builder, Major Leonard Vassall, who had begun its construction in 1731.

Though she was often far away from Quincy, her instructions and plans for her home were imaginatively conceived and meticulously thought out. The construction of the large extension at one end of the house which includes the long room, the east entry and the upstairs study, was directed by mail.

*Above:* The Adams Old House is a pleasant, colonial-style house with gabled, mansard roof and gray clapboards. *Right:* The most charming feature of the Presidents' Bedroom is the fireplace from Liverpool.

John Adams lived on twenty-six years after his term in Presidential office. At Quincy, he read Horace and Livy, put his papers in order, served as president of the American Academy of Arts and Sciences. He bought more land, painted apple trees to discourage the tent caterpillars, and supervised the carting of seaweed to fertilize the fields.

The Adams home is recognized, not surprisingly, as having permanent historic interest; in 1947 Abigail's cherished Quincy, filled with family heirlooms and paintings, its nearly five acres including the library, garden and stables, was given to the Federal Government by the Adams Memorial Society. Now the public may visit the home of this astonishing family who have served their country and their fellow men as diplomats, writers and ambassadors, apparently with tireless dedication.

# LONGFELLOW HOUSE
## *The Poet's "Italian Villa"*

When Henry Wadsworth Longfellow, poet and professor of modern languages at Harvard University, left his room at Mrs. Stearn's, mainly because he could not "endure boarding homes," he moved into "two large and beautiful rooms" in the Craigie house, Cambridge, Massachusetts, where he hoped to be "entirely my own master, and have my meals by myself and at my own hours." "I form to myself a vision of independence," he wrote to his father. What Longfellow could not possibly have envisioned at that moment was that he had moved into the Craigie house for the remaining forty-five years of his life, to live there with his wife and five children and to write some of his most memorable poems there. One day he would have the house named and preserved in his honor.

Longfellow married Fanny Appleton in July 1843, and was given the Craigie house by his father-in-law that autumn, a much appreciated present. It reposed on five acres and the Charles River wound through the meadows in front. Longfellow planted an avenue of linden trees behind the house.

What is the Longfellow House today and was once Mrs. Andrew Craigie's house, has a hold on the historical past that dates back to before the American Revolution. It was built in 1759 by Major John Vassall whose grandfather had built the house in Quincy that was bought later by John Adams.

The house served as a hospital after the Battle of Bunker Hill, and still later, it housed Colonel John Glover's "amphibious regiment" of Marblehead fishermen, an event that has caused some people to consider Longfellow's house as the "first headquarters of the American navy." It is the events, however, of the time between July 1775 and March 1776, that provide Longfellow House with its most inspired historical moments. George Washington arrived in Cambridge to take command of the continental forces and made the John Vassal house his headquarters.

Today, sitting atop a double terrace facing south, the imposing two-storied frame house displays an expansive hip roof containing four outstanding elements: a massive yellow chimney at either end, a white balustraded widow's walk, a white-trimmed pediment with delicate fanlight in the center of the front and flanking the pediment, two rather large dormers.

The hallway runs through to the Blue Entry in back which connects with the ell. It and the front staircase, as well as all the other first-floor rooms, have white-painted wainscoting. The parlor to the left of the hall has served history hospitably on many occasions, welcoming leaders of the Revolution as well as Prince Talleyrand and the Emperor of Brazil.

Longfellow's study, directly across the hall from the parlor, was Washington's dining room. The portraits on the wall include one of Nathaniel Hawthorne, Longfellow's classmate at Bowdoin, and one of Emerson by Eastman Johnson. The heavy ornate chair at the right of the fireplace is made out of the wood of the "spreading chestnut tree" which Longfellow had referred to in his poem "The Village Blacksmith." It was a gift in 1879 from the schoolchildren of Cambridge.

*Opposite:* Longfellow lived in his handsome Georgian-style house with flair and affluence.
*Below:* The five Louis XVI armchairs in the parlor are of carved walnut. (Louis H. Frohman Photos)

# OLD MANSE
## The House of Emerson and Hawthorne

From this home in Concord, Massachusetts, on April 19, 1775, Ralph Waldo Emerson's grandfather, the Reverend William Emerson, watched the firing of the famous "shot heard round the world" which his grandson was later to immortalize. The sage of New England Transcendentalism spent part of his boyhood in the house on Monument Street. The most famous occupant of the house, however, was Nathaniel Hawthorne, who brought his bride to the Old Manse in 1842 for a four-year stay.

It is a two-and-a-half-story clapboard structure with a gambrel roof and two pedimented doorways. For its day it was a large house. There are four rooms and a central hall downstairs, in addition to the usual sheds in the rear. On the second floor there are four bedrooms and the third floor has several small chambers for visitors, including one room known as the "saints chamber," kept for the use of visiting clergymen.

The Old Manse, built in 1769 and remaining today essentially the same as when the Reverend William Emerson moved into it, was turned over to the state-controlled Trustees of Reservations in 1939.

The Old Manse provided shelter for the imaginative spirits of Ralph Waldo Emerson and Nathaniel Hawthorne.

John Greenleaf Whittier may have sat and warmed himself before the large fireplace of his New England homestead.

# JOHN GREENLEAF WHITTIER HOMESTEAD
## *Home of "Snow-Bound"*

"The sun that brief December day ... Rose cheerless over hills of gray...." The opening lines of John Greenleaf Whittier's famous winter idyl, "Snow-Bound," have been familiar to students for well over a century. The word picture of life on a New England farm during a driving storm is a classic of American literature and certainly the best known of Whittier's many poems.

The house which it describes is still standing in Haverhill, Massachusetts, and on a winter's day one can stand on its grounds and imagine the giant drifts and the boys of the family tunneling their way to the barn to feed the animals, and the stories told around the fire as the family awaited the end of the fury.

The Whittier Homestead was built by Thomas Whittier in 1688. It was here that the poet, a great-great-grandson of Thomas, was born on December 17, 1807. The house is much the same as when Whittier knew it during the years when he was growing up. The large fireplace in the kitchen is easily recognized as the one mentioned in "Snow-Bound." The elevated Mother's Bedroom, built over a rock too large to move, is still to be seen and many of the furnishings, including Whittier's desk, are still in place.

Outside is the natural stone mounting-block used by generations of children and the doorstone on which the "Barefoot Boy" ate his bowl of milk and bread.

11

The Nathan Hale House in Coventry
is classic Early American architecture. (Louis H. Frohman Photo)

# NATHAN HALE HOUSE
## *Home to a Patriot's Family*

In 1776, Nathan Hale, the schoolmaster turned revolutionary soldier and spy, was hanged by the British and his famous last words indelibly recorded in history, "I only regret that I have but one life to give for my country."

After his death, Nathan's family moved into a new house on South Street in Coventry, Connecticut, which is now an official memorial to the valiant young schoolmaster and, in a larger sense, to the Puritan family that produced him. Shortly after their move, the smaller adjacent structure, where Hale had been born, was pulled down.

The clapboard is a classic example of the Early American architecture, simple and severe — with an austere beauty nevertheless. Two and a half stories tall, with gable roofs, it has two chimneys over the main section and two over the ell. There are no over-

hangs or architectural ornamentation, but the clapboards are graduated, narrow above the baseboard, increasing in width above. Part of the ell was built at the same time as the main portion, and the north wall of the old house, Hale's birthplace, was grafted to the south side of the ell. Several years were required to finish the interiors, and the fine paneling and woodwork reflect changes of taste and the work of various craftsmen.

The fabrics on display in the house are unusual. Most of them are original materials, some of which were found in trunks in the attic.

The simplicity of the homestead, which also displays a considerable degree of refinement and craftsmanship for its time and place, reflects the character of the Hale family and of the son and brother who died a hero.

# JONATHAN TRUMBULL HOUSE

## First Among the Patriots

Connecticut Yankee Jonathan Trumbull was a prosperous merchant and an important political figure during Revolutionary times. He was to be the only colonial governor to side with the colonies in the war. Beginning soon after the Battle of Lexington in Massachusetts, Trumbull and his sons and son-in-law began furnishing supplies to the Continental Army and dispatching troops.

Frequent conferences occurred in Trumbull's home between John Adams, Thomas Jefferson, John Jay, Lafayette and Washington. Washington stated that "but for Jonathan Trumbull, the war could not have been carried to a successful conclusion," and said he was "among the first patriots."

Of his children, John, the artist, was perhaps the most remarkable. John's special contribution during the War of Independence was to sketch plans of the British works.

The Trumbull House in Lebanon, which was a considerable mansion for its time and place, now belongs to the Connecticut Daughters of the American Revolution. After it passed from the family, it was moved by yoke of oxen to its present pleasant location. Standing two and a half stories, the austere white-painted frame dwelling is surmounted by a steep gable roof with a massive square chimney rising from the center.

Kitchen display includes pewter plates and spinning wheel. (J. Linton Houser Photo, FPG)

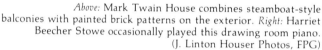
*Above:* Mark Twain House combines steamboat-style balconies with painted brick patterns on the exterior. *Right:* Harriet Beecher Stowe occasionally played this drawing room piano. (J. Linton Houser Photos, FPG)

# MARK TWAIN HOUSE
## *"Part Steamboat, Part Medieval Stronghold"*

To a passerby pausing at 351 Farmington Avenue in Hartford, Connecticut, in 1874, the new three-storied residence of Samuel L. Clemens, more renowned as Mark Twain, and his wife Olivia, was "one of the oddest buildings in the state ever designed for a dwelling, if not in the whole country." A year after Clemens' marriage to Olivia Langdon of Elmira, New York, the couple decided to settle among friends such as Isabella Beecher Stowe, half-sister of Harriet Beecher Stowe, in Nook Farm Colony, a section of Hartford favored by artists and writers. Edward

Tuckerman Potter of New York, who had designed the Church of the Heavenly Rest, was hired to draw plans for the house which took more than a year to complete for a most impatient and changeable client.

This unique house was "part steamboat, part medieval stronghold, and part cuckoo clock," nineteen rooms and five baths inside a brick house patterned in black and scarlet, festooned with balconies, turrets and porches, and trimmed with fern-bearing flower boxes every angle of the way. The interior, decorated in 1881 mainly by Louis Comfort Tiffany, lived up to

the promise of the exterior. One could safely say Tiffany caught the spirit of the architect and spared nothing — not a stenciled wall, not a stained-glass window, not a glass tile.

It was in the billiard room of his Hartford house in the winter and Quarry Farm, Elmira, in the summer that Clemens wrote *The Adventures of Huckleberry Finn*, *The Adventures of Tom Sawyer*, *The Prince and the Pauper* and *A Connecticut Yankee at King Arthur's Court*. He was described by his friend William Dean Howells, "at the crest of the prosperity which enabled him to humor every whim or extravagance."

In 1929, the Mark Twain Library and Memorial Commission bought the home, renting out portions to the public library. The house stands today as a remarkable memorial to the man Mark Twain and to the gilded age in which he lived. The rooms have been furnished appropriately for the period and the family's taste. Particular care has been given to the restoration of the interior decor. Not far away in the illustrious neighborhood, the Harriet Beecher Stowe House can be seen.

15

*Above:* Jones never owned the patrician house bearing his name, though he roomed here two different times. *Opposite:* Fine Sheraton chest boasts serpentine front and ball-and-claw feet. (Hans Wendler Photos, FPG)

# JOHN PAUL JONES HOUSE
## *Where the Dashing Captain Waited*

The most romantic and controversial American naval figure, John Paul Jones, was born in Scotland, served in Russia, died in France and is reburied at Annapolis. But he is remembered in the sea town of Portsmouth, New Hampshire, by having the house where he boarded renamed in his honor. It was at Mrs. Purcell's on Middle and State streets, now called the John Paul Jones House, where he lived in the best front bedchamber during the year 1777 while the sloop of war *Ranger* was being built at Langdon's Island and where he returned in 1781 while he supervised the construction of the seventy-four-gun ship *America.*

The John Paul Jones House holds its own nobly in this town of distinguished dwellings. It is one of the finest examples of frame houses built by many leading citizens during the eighteenth century. Standing two and a half stories with pedimented lintels over the first-floor windows and the third-floor end dormers, the house has been expanded a number of times over the years, which is also typical of many Portsmouth houses. In 1973 it was designated a national historic landmark.

Today the house is furnished with many interesting pieces of period furniture and collections of objects brought back from the Orient by New England sailors. Filling a large part of the space in the bedroom which Jones occupied are models of ships built in Portsmouth, a copy of the flag John Paul Jones flew and a letter written by him. Here also a model of the *Ranger,* the ship that originally caused the dashing hero to come to Portsmouth.

# BLAINE HOUSE
*Imposing Mansion of the "Plumed Knight"*

*Below:* A gracefully curving staircase ascends to the second floor from the entrance hall.
*Opposite:* Since 1920, Blaine House has provided fifteen state governors and their families with a vast, precisely furnished house. (Photos: Courtesy Maine Department of Economic Development)

For her birthday in 1862, Harriet Standwood Blaine's husband, James Gillespie Blaine, deeded her a "mansion house" and her share, like that of so many wives of political figures, of two lives, one "all variety, wide-awake, gay; the other all Aunt Susan, sewing machine, children." Since then the Blaine House in Augusta, Maine, has been the setting for many notable occasions and dramatic events.

While a member of Congress, Blaine was a member of all its principal committees. Beginning in 1862, he served fourteen years in the House of Representatives, three times as speaker. The fourteenth amendment of the Constitution, giving citizenship to everyone born in the United States, passed during Reconstruction, was "substantially" Blaine's proposition.

Blaine lost the Presidential nomination in 1880 and the office itself the next time around mainly because he was deserted by the Independent Republicans, who were called "the Mugwumps." The continuing shadow cast by a charge of graft was the final cause of the distrust that smogged Blaine's name.

He was exonerated by the House, and though there were the staunch followers who thought of Blaine as "a plumed knight" marching down the halls of the American Congress to throw his "shining lance full and fair against . . . the maligners of his honor," the opposition party's limerick haunts his name to this day: "Blaine, Blaine, James G. Blaine, Continental liar from the State of Maine."

By 1872 the Blaines added a conservatory, combined the sitting and dining room into a large family dining room (now the State Dining Room), enclosed the veranda, added a cupola and brought up five children.

In 1893, James G. Blaine died of Bright's disease; Blaine House passed into Harriet Blaine Beale's possession and was given to her son Walker. When Walker died in battle in 1919 in France, Mrs. Beale gave the house to the State of Maine.

19

# WADSWORTH-LONGFELLOW HOUSE
## *Where a Famed Poet Was Nurtured*

Henry Wadsworth Longfellow's poem, "My Lost Youth," conveys the essential happiness of his boyhood and youth in Portland, Maine. In this now quiet seaport town, there still stands the venerable brick house where America's most beloved poet lived during his infancy, boyhood and young manhood, where he wrote his first poems, where he decided on a literary career, and where he often visited until his death in 1882 at the age of seventy-five years. That dwelling is the Wadsworth-Longfellow House, built 183 years ago by the poet's maternal grandfather, General Peleg Wadsworth, an adjutant general of the Massachusetts militia during the American Revolution. The house is now owned by the Maine Historical Society.

The front parlor is furnished entirely with Longfellow family pieces including the piano that belonged to the poet while he was at Cambridge. (Photos: permission granted by Maine Historical Society)

Bronze furniture in the Marble House dining room is set against dark pink marble walls.
(Preservation Society of Newport County Photos)

# MARBLE HOUSE
## *The Vanderbilts' Age of Ostentation*

Bellevue Avenue in Newport, Rhode Island, was shrouded by fog the night of August 19, 1892, when suddenly all the lights of Marble House, both gas and electric, were turned on and one of the great spectacles in the history of Newport began. Mr. and Mrs. William K. Vanderbilt had opened their sumptuous new mansion to their friends for the first time, and the visitors were overwhelmed. It was soon acknowledged to be one of the finest houses to be built during this period, sometimes called the American Renaissance.

Richard Morris Hunt — who had designed The Breakers for Mr. Vanderbilt's brother Cornelius, the famous financier — designed Marble House in the fashion of Louis XIV, who was greatly admired by both Mr. and Mrs. Vanderbilt. Some say that the White House played a part in Hunt's inspiration, while others mention the Petit Trianon at Versailles. In any

Marble House was named for the wide variety of marble used in its construction.

case it is lavish throughout, in a summer resort noted for its lavish homes, many of which were built after Marble House.

Ostentatious decoration is to be found throughout the entire first floor of the mansion and reaches even to the bedrooms on the second floor.

In 1895 the house was the scene of a magnificent party honoring the debut of Consuelo Vanderbilt, who later became the Duchess of Marlborough. A year later the Vanderbilts were divorced and Mrs.

Vanderbilt married O. H. P. Belmont. After his death in 1908, she returned to Marble House, which had been closed for 12 years, and that summer gave a garden party to which the public was invited. It was to promote the cause of woman suffrage.

In 1932 the house was sold to Frederick H. Prince of Boston, and it remained in his family until 1963 when it was bought from his trust by the Preservation Society of Newport County.

The Gothic Room marks an abrupt departure from the seventeenth- and eighteenth-century French style which is dominant throughout the rest of the Marble House.

# JOHN JAY HOMESTEAD
*Rambling Farmhouse of the First Chief Justice*

Hanging in the front parlor is a compelling portrait of Jay in the robes of Chief Justice. (Pendor Natural Color Photos)

Modest and comfortable, the John Jay Homestead was expanded into a gracious shelter.

John Jay occupied exactly two rooms as United States Secretary of Foreign Affairs and a study made by a Congressional committee in 1788 reveals that records and papers could be reached without "delay or difficulty....Upon the whole...neatness, method and perspicuity" were evident throughout the department. It would not take another Congressional committee to apply the same description to the Jay Homestead that John Jay built in Bedford, New York. Two-story, modest, comfortable, painted gray-green with sienna shutters, the farmhouse has been expanded over the years into a gracious shelter for generations that have included another judge, as well as a Minister to Austria.

Jay was aristocratic, conservative and a strong nationalist. Paradoxically, he was also visionary and liberal. He was a member of the first Continental Congress and eventually its president. He was an emissary to Spain, Secretary of State for Foreign Affairs after the Revolution, first Chief Justice under the new Constitution and New York's governor from 1795 to 1801 when he retired to Bedford where he lived until 1829.

Major alterations and additions on the Jay farmhouse, which had originally been built from 200,-000 bricks ordered to be done at the building site and completed in 1787, did not begin until 1800. Of the five rooms that comprised the original farmhouse, three of them — the front parlor and dining room in the front and the Victorian parlor in the rear — are off a central hall, while the library adjoins the Victorian parlor and the Red Kitchen is off a small hallway in the rear of the house.

Richly embellished by time and many sophisticated purchases, today the house is a fascinating gallery of portraits of America's innovators, including DeWitt Clinton, inventor and governor of New York, painted by Ezra Ames, and Timothy Dwight, president of Yale College, by John Trumbull.

John Jay's house was lived in by his family until it was bought by Westchester County and presented to New York State as an historic site in 1958 and restored and opened to the public in 1964 as a tribute to an esteemed American. Jay has his own ideas on this subject: "The esteem of the estimable is certainly of great value, but the transient praise of the multitude, like feathers blown on and off by the passing breeze, can weigh but little."

The angular, twenty-three-room mansion stands on a site
exposed to the strong winds of Long Island Sound. (Sondak Photos, FPG)

# SAGAMORE HILL
## A Rough Rider's Victorian Retreat

Sagamore Hill in Oyster Bay, Long Island, New York, is exactly the type of house one would associate with President Theodore Roosevelt. The rambling twenty-three-room Victorian dwelling, even from the outside, is a projection of his personality. Inside, there could be no doubt as to the family who lived there.

Designed by Roosevelt himself and built in the 1880's, the house was named Sagamore Hill for the Indian chief who ceded the land to the first settlers.

The first floor of the house's exterior is brick, the second and third floors are clapboarded. Standing on a site exposed to the strong winds of Long Island Sound, the house is solidly built, with foundations twenty inches thick. Roosevelt's beloved and spacious piazza looks out from the south and west sides of the house over Oyster Bay Harbor.

*(continued on p. 28)*

A pastel portrait of Mrs. Roosevelt by Philip Laszlo is displayed in her drawing room. An Aubusson rug covers the floor.

*Above:* In the momentous North Room, Roosevelt's portrait is surmounted by a carved eagle crafted by Gutzon Borglum. *Below:* Roosevelt's children and their cousins enjoyed themselves at Sagamore HIll: They swam, skated in winter and served tea to their teddy bears.

Among the rooms on the first floor is the Trophy Room, or North Room, which was added in 1904-05 when Roosevelt felt the need to expand in order to accommodate the many visitors to the summer White House. It is a momentous room, thirty feet wide and forty feet long, both impressive and personal, ornamented with columns of Philippine mahogany and stuffed with treasures.

In 1950 the house and eighty-three acres of land were purchased by the Roosevelt Memorial Association and donated to the Federal Government in 1962. The house is completely restored as authentically as possible, with the help of relatives' memory and actual documents, to its peak Victorian comfort.

# OLANA
## *Frederick Church's Moorish Castle On the Hudson River*

Olana, a Moorish castle near the town of Hudson, New York, was built and furnished by Frederick Edwin Church, landscape artist of the Hudson River School. All of his ability is evident in this thirty-seven room attraction, for the materials used in its construction utilize light in all ways to reflect or silhouette. The house ranks as one of the most sophisticated Victorian creations still extant in three ways — historically, artistically and architecturally. In addition to the artifacts on display from Church's worldwide journeys are many of his realistic landscapes.

Built in 1870-72, the stone and brick house has many features that seem to suggest eccentricity: pointed arches, protruding balconies, a four-story bell tower. Eastern motifs are repeated around the exterior with colorful inlaid tile.

After passing through the front door, shaped like a Persian arch, one is overwhelmed by architectural furnishings and details that bear out the proud builder's description of the house: "Persian adapted to Occident." Door panels have stenciled Arabic patterns. Many of the carpets are from Syria. The porcelains are Persian. In the dining room, which is also a picture gallery, Duncan Phyfe furniture mixes with Italian Victorian and antique Turkish.

Church, known as the "Michelangelo of landscape art," often painted scenes of the Hudson River. One view of the great river that he rendered many times can be seen from the mammoth picture window in the court hall that looks beyond a recessed porch.

The castle with its lavish yet functional furnishings is administered by the State of New York and has been declared a national historical landmark.

Olana, home of artist Frederick Church, is a mansion of eye-catching individuality, having Moorish windows surrounded by colorful patterns.
(Charles P. Noyes Photo)

29

# FRANKLIN D. ROOSEVELT HOME
## An Old-Fashioned Home

Hyde Park, New York, was the home of Franklin Delano Roosevelt from the day he was born. No matter where he went — to Campobello Island in Nova Scotia, the White House or Warm Springs, Georgia — he always considered the house at the edge of a gently rolling plateau overlooking the Hudson River as home.

The future President of the United States was born at Hyde Park on January 30, 1882, the only child of James and Sara Delano Roosevelt. At that time the house, which had been built about 1826, and purchased by James in 1867, was a frame dwelling.

It was here that he brought his bride, Eleanor, in 1905, and here that their children were raised. It was from Hyde Park that he started on the political trail that led to the Presidency of the United States. And it is here that he is buried.

The house has undergone many alterations since James Roosevelt purchased it. The original clapboards were removed and the walls were covered with stucco. The front of the house was completely changed to include a sweeping balustrade and a colonnaded portico. On each end of the old portion of the house two-story wings were added, creating an H-shaped structure.

The portico is well known to all Americans and to many from foreign lands. It was at Hyde Park that F.D.R. welcomed his neighbors and friends when he returned from gaining the Democratic nomination for the Presidency in 1932 — and it was here that he was cheered by his Dutchess County friends on four triumphant election nights. Here he met the King and Queen of England in 1939, and later Prime Minister Winston Churchill and other world leaders.

The family's way of life and the interests of three generations are immediately evident from the furnishings and decorations of the house. In the large rectangular front hall are a few large pieces of furniture and the walls are covered with part of one of the finest collections of naval prints in existence. Directly across from the entrance door is an 18th-century grandfather's clock and to the left of the door is a massive oak wardrobe. Both pieces were bought in the Netherlands by Roosevelt's parents while on their wedding trip in 1881. To the left of the clock is a sideboard acquired in Italy by James in 1869. The room also contains a wall case with many of the birds young Franklin collected as a boy.

The rooms on the second floor give more evidence of a comfortable, old-fashioned way of living without pretense or ostentation.

Throughout the turmoil of public and political life, President Franklin Roosevelt often turned to the restful, refreshing surroundings of his ancestral home at Hyde Park, New York. (National Park Service Photo)

*Above:* Sunnyside, Washington Irving's picturesque nineteenth-century home in New York, reflects the whimsy and romanticism of the renowned author. (Epstein Photo, FPG) *Opposite, above:* During the first ten years of his occupancy, Irving used the study virtually as a one-room apartment, doing most of his writing here. (CB Photo)

# SUNNYSIDE
## *European Romanticism on the Hudson*

Washington Irving's picturesque, nineteenth-century home, Sunnyside, stands on a high bank of the Hudson River at Tarrytown, but bears little resemblance to the seventeenth-century Dutch cottage which the famed American author purchased in 1835. Looking at it himself after he had made a series of changes, he described it as "a little old-fashioned stone mansion, all made up of gable ends, and as full of angles and corners as an old cocked hat."

Despite his rather facetious description, Sunnyside has a charm all its own. Beautifully landscaped grounds with flowers growing in profusion, quiet glens and sheltering groves surround the house. There is also a duck pond, which Irving called his "Lit-tle Mediterranean," and a waterfall. Nearby are the service buildings: the woodshed, root cellar and a steepled ice house.

His study, on the right of the central hall, was often the scene of lively literary discussions and the huge desk, the chairs, the massive bookcases, containing his library, are there today. Also there is a daybed in a draped alcove which was used by Irving nightly for the first ten years he lived at Sunnyside when the house was overflowing with relatives and friends. The parlor, on the left rear, was the center of family life. At the far end of the parlor is a picture gallery containing many of the original drawings done by famous artists to illustrate Irving's works.

# WILLIAM H. SEWARD HOUSE
*Home of a Great Statesman*

The home is a pleasing combination of Federal- and
Tuscan-style architecture. William Henry Seward lived here for almost fifty years.
(Photos: courtesy Foundation Historical Association, Inc.)

A family gallery of portraits line one wall of the drawing room.

Still standing on its original site in the central New York town of Auburn and now more than 150 years old, the Seward House is a worthy memorial to one of America's greatest statesmen. As Secretary of State under President Lincoln, he skillfully guided this country's foreign relations during the crucial years of the Civil War. Before the war, Seward had served as a New York State Senator, as governor of the state, and as a United States Senator for twelve years.

The Seward house was built in the then popular Federal style in 1816-1817 by Seward's father-in-law, Judge Elijah Miller. Seward, a junior law partner of the judge, married the judge's daughter Frances in 1824. Before the marriage, Judge Miller, a widower with two daughters, stipulated that his future son-in-law should live in the house with the family. This was agreed to by the young lawyer, and it was his home for nearly fifty years, during the time he achieved his greatest renown as an anti-slavery leader, one of the founders of the Republican party, a United States

Senator, Presidential aspirant, and finally as Secretary of State in the cabinets of President Lincoln and President Johnson.

It was during this period, too, that he entertained in his Auburn residence some of the most distinguished men of his era. Among them were Presidents John Quincy Adams, Martin Van Buren and Andrew Johnson, and General Ulysses S. Grant, George Custer, Admiral David Farragut and Henry Clay. Here, too, was his permanent home when, in 1850, he made his famous anti-slavery declarations.

After his death in 1872, the Seward mansion was occupied by a son, General William Henry Seward II, who had served in the Civil War. When he died in 1920, the historic landmark became the property and home of William Henry Seward III. At his death in 1951, the house passed into the hands of The Foundation Historical Association of Auburn, a group formed to preserve Seward's residence as a memorial to one of the greatest Secretaries of State in American history.

35

# FORD MANSION
## *Washington's Headquarters,*
## *Landmark of the Revolution*

*Below:* The room used by General and Mrs. Washington has the original secretary-desk where he wrote his dispatches. *Opposite:* The Ford Mansion has been described as a "wooden Palladian mansion of the Dutch-English transition." (J. Linton Houser Photos, FPG)

In December of 1779, General George Washington set up winter quarters in an ample, gracious white house, four miles from the heart of Morristown, New Jersey, at the invitation of its mistress, Mrs. Jacob Ford, Jr., and he stayed until spring.

Jacob Ford, Jr., one of the pioneers of the iron business, was "no doubt the leading man in Morristown," and when the house was completed in 1774, it was considered the town's finest residence.

Upon the death of Jacob Ford's grandson, Henry A. Ford, in 1873, Ford Mansion was purchased for $25,000 by four New Jersey citizens who organized the Washington Association of New Jersey to preserve the structure. For nearly sixty years after the house was opened to the public, this group collected many of the outstanding furnishings, manuscripts and art objects now in the house. In 1933 the association gave Ford Mansion to the Federal Government as a part of the Morristown National Historical Park and six years later the restoration to the 1779-1780 period was completed.

The Ford Mansion has been rather formidably described as a "wooden Palladian mansion of the Dutch-English transition," built in the style of Inigo Jones, who has sometimes been called the "English Palladio." The two-and-a-half-story main section is surmounted by a dentil cornice and hipped roof, flanked by two large square chimneys. But the chief feature of the exterior is the elaborately decorated Palladian doorway with a more restrained second-story Palladian window directly over it. The main section has a central hall flanked by two rooms on each side, and the two-story east wing contains the kitchen and buttery and servants' rooms above.

To the left, the large room used by General and Mrs. Washington as both a living and dining room contains the original secretary-desk where he wrote his dispatches.

Across the hall is the combination living and dining room where Mrs. Ford lived with her family during the time the mansion was used as Washington's headquarters.

As Washington noted, it was the kitchen in the east wing, a large room and the warmest one in the house, that served as a gathering place during the coldest days that historic winter. It is now completely furnished with colonial utensils and cooking tools and the banister-back armchair is a Ford family piece that was here at the time.

When Walt Whitman took over this home he had to furnish it with boxes for tables and chairs. (Historical Pictures Service Photo)

# WALT WHITMAN HOUSE
## *Order Amid Chaos*

The house in Camden, New Jersey, has nothing to recommend it architecturally. The two-story frame structure with six cramped rooms was built for a lower middle-class working man of the mid-19th century.

In the 1880's the entire neighborhood consisted of working men, their broods of children — and one immortal figure, Walt Whitman. Here in his declining years he found peace and contentment, and while the distinguished personalities who visited him might have wondered about the surroundings, Whitman appeared to most to be unaware of anything being amiss about his place of residence.

An English visitor described his room on the second floor as partly carpeted and heated by a little stove: "All around him were books, manuscripts, letters, papers, magazines, parcels tied up with bits of string, photographs and literary material, which was piled a yard high, filled two or three wastepaper baskets, flowed over them to the floor, beneath the table, on to and under the chairs, bed, washstands, etc., so that whenever he moved from his chair he had literally to wade through this sea of chaotic disorder and confusion."

But Whitman could immediately put his hand on whatever he wanted in this chaos. His sense of order was in his mind and his poetry.

In 1920 the house was purchased from some Whitman relatives by a group who represented the City of Camden. It was turned into a museum which contains the original furnishings, pictures and memorabilia of Whitman.

# THOMPSON-NEELY HOUSE
## *Washington's "House of Decision"*

The plans for the audacious and successful Christmas Night attack, 1776, on Trenton by crossing the Delaware River were formulated in a Bucks County, Pennsylvania farmhouse — the Thompson-Neely House — by Washington and members of his staff.

Brigadier General William Alexander, titular Earl of Stirling, who had sided with the American cause, was headquartered at the house. It was here that Washington had to consider what would happen to his ill-equipped army if he dragged it into battle with the British in mid-winter. After intense talks, the decision was made — and the house became known as "The House of Decision."

The original section of the Thompson-Neely House was a one-room stone cabin built in 1702. The west end of the house consisting of two stories was added in 1757. A few years later a second story was added to the original part and, in 1788, the east end was built.

Robert Thompson acquired the property around 1748. His daughter married a William Neely and both families occupied the house at the time of the Revolution. Descendants remained in possession of the property until 1880. From that time until 1926, when the Commonwealth of Pennsylvania purchased it, the property was privately owned.

The Council Room of the Thompson-Neely House. (Yeager and Kay Photo)

The rear of Pennsbury Manor is flanked by the bake-and-brew house.
(Pennsylvania Historical and Museum Commission Photos)

# PENNSBURY MANOR
## *William Penn's Manor*

William Penn came to America with perhaps the most idealistic plans of any of those who left the religiously distraught shores of Europe. He was seeking a place not only for the members of the Society of Friends but for any and all who were non-conformists in England, France, Holland, Germany and Ireland.

In 1683 the site for Penn's home in the New World was chosen. It was located on the Delaware River, in Lower Bucks County, about twenty-five miles north of Philadelphia, Pennsylvania. As might be expected, he planned the house, the surrounding buildings and the gardens after the fashion of the English and Irish manor houses to which he was accustomed. Many of the original materials were brought from England, but the bricks and timbers are believed to have been shaped locally.

Penn had hoped to make the manor his home for the rest of his life, but political and personal affairs in London forced him to return in 1684 and he did not see the manor again until 1699. He remained in this country for one year, returning again to London.

The Penns owned this land until about the time of the Revolutionary War. After the Penns departed the manor fell into semi-ruin. In the early 1930's a group met and set up plans to restore the famed homestead of the founder of the state. Through their efforts and those of others the stately mansion now stands again on the shores of the Delaware a fitting tribute to that idealistic man, William Penn.

Interior displays crude implements of the settlers and medicinal herbs hanging from exposed beams.

The residence of John Dickinson originally had a hipped roof which was ruined by fire and replaced by the gable roof. (Courtesy Delaware State Development Department Photo)

# JOHN DICKINSON MANSION
## *"The Penman of the Revolution"*

Some five miles southeast of Delaware's capital city of Dover stands the old colonial home of John Dickinson, known in American history as "The Penman of the Revolution." An early writer once said of him: "In the literature of that struggle, his position is as preeminent as Washington in war, Franklin in diplomacy and Morris in finance."

Although he served as governor of both Delaware and Pennsylvania (the chief executive of the two colonies was then known as President), John Dickinson did not come from either of them. He was born in Maryland. John's father acquired a large tract of land in Kent County, Delaware, and when John was

eight years old, the family moved into a brick mansion built by his father in 1740 on the Delaware land, the house that now is one of the outstanding historic landmarks of Delaware.

His influence grew wide with the publication, in 1768, of his famous *Letters of a Farmer in Pennsylvania* and, in the same year, *A Song for American Freedom*. Both dealt with the colonists and their rights as free men. Later he drafted the "Petition to the King" and "Address to the Inhabitants of Quebec" adopted by the Congress of 1774. With the outbreak of the American Revolution, however, John Dickinson exchanged his pen for a sword, and served as a colonel in the Continental

Covering the bed in the main chamber is a spread depicting General Washington and thirteen patriots, one of whom is John Dickinson. (Courtesy Delaware State Archives, Hall of Records Photo)

Army and later as a brigadier general in the Delaware Militia.

Regarded as a fine example of lower Delaware eighteenth-century, plantation architecture, the two-story Dickinson Mansion has its brickwork laid in Flemish bond. Originally, the house had a hip roof, but this was ruined when fire attacked the upper part of the dwelling in 1804. In repairing and restoring his country manor, John Dickinson added to it a gable roof. At an earlier period, a dining room wing and a kitchen wing were built onto the house. Re-creation of the original Dickinson gardens has been undertaken by various Delaware garden clubs.

Built more than two centuries ago, the John Dickinson house would have been destroyed had it not been for prompt action on the part of the National Society of the Colonial Dames of America in the State of Delaware. It was in 1952 that the society, realizing the historic importance of the house, donated $25,000 to the State of Delaware for its purchase and preservation, and the state matched this gift. Since then, a special committee has furnished the landmark with period pieces, some of them from the Pennsylvania-Delaware region. The house is now maintained as a public museum.

# THE WHITE HOUSE
## *Home of Presidents*

*Above:* The White House has been in a state of change almost from the moment James Hoban designed it. *Right:* A mahogany secretary in the Green Room. *Opposite:* The green silk damask walls gave the Federal-style Green Room its name. (All photos: Copyright by White House Historical Association, photos by National Geographic Society)

In the more than a century and a half that it has been the official residence of the Presidents of the United States, the White House has undergone many changes, some necessitated by fire, some to meet expanding needs, some to meet changing conventions and, during President Truman's administration, to save the building from collapse.

The main part of the residence is essentially the same as was designed by the Irish-born architect James Hoban, who was given the commission in 1792. The White House is the most distinguished residence in the United States and, set among trees and shrubs and well manicured lawns, it is considered the center of the affairs of the non-Communist world, as well as the home of the President and his family.

It is magnificent without being flamboyant. It is dignified, yet it has found room for the romping of children through its halls, as well as the more sedate pace of distinguished guests from all corners of the globe.

When Hoban was given the task of designing the residence, the commissioners for the Federal City expected that it would be ready when the Government moved there in 1800. However, when John Adams and his wife, Abigail, moved in they found the house far from finished.

When Thomas Jefferson moved into the Executive Mansion in 1801, he found the house "big enough for two emperors, one Pope and the Grand Lama." Jefferson called in Benjamin Henry Latrobe, a renowned architect and designer of the time, in an effort to complete the mansion.

With each changing administration, changing personalities and changing times, the White House took on some of the personality of the latest occupant. Furnishings were acquired from many sources and paintings, sculpture and silver were added to enhance the residence.

The interior of the White House has always been impressive, but in recent years it seems to have taken on an air of quiet dignity in keeping with the nation's role in the world.

*Above:* A bronze doré fruit basket is one of the mansion's greatest treasures.
*Opposite:* The table in the State Dining Room is ornamented by superb bronze doré pieces.

*Above:* The high-columned piazza stretching across Mount Vernon's river front is believed to be unique for its period. *Opposite:* The Palladian window in the Banquet Hall is decorated with Adamesque ornament. (Photos: courtesy Mt. Vernon Ladies' Assoc.)

# MOUNT VERNON
## *Washington's Lavish Country Seat*

"No estate in United America is more pleasantly situated than this. It lies in a high, dry and healthy country three hundred miles by water from the sea."

Thus George Washington described the estate of Mount Vernon in Virginia in a letter to an English correspondent. Time and circumstance have done little to change the Mount Vernon he loved. It stands as a monument to the builder, "pleasantly situated" on a commanding eminence overlooking the Potomac and the low Maryland hills on the opposite shore.

Mount Vernon is an outstanding example of colonial architecture. It is unique in many ways and owes its charm more to harmony of composition than to the beauty of its component parts. Washington had access to eighteenth-century English books on the design of country houses; the Palladian window and other details of the house, interior and exterior, were copied or derived from one or more of these books.

The most striking architectural feature of the mansion is the high-columned piazza, extending the full length of the house. It seems to be a complete innovation, and would, in itself, entitle Washington to distinction among architects.

In Washington's day, the Mount Vernon estate of over 8,000 acres was divided into five farms, each a complete unit, with its overseer, workers, livestock,

equipment and buildings. Washington was one of the most progressive farmers of his day, despite the major diversions created by his public service.

During the half century following Washington's death in 1799, Mount Vernon's owners were unable to maintain its buildings and grounds. Neither the State of Virginia nor the Federal Government expressed an interest in the property. But in 1853, just as it looked as if the estate might crumble into ruins, a woman from South Carolina, Ann Pamela Cunning-ham, became interested in its preservation and devoted the next twenty-one years of her life to the project. To her and the Mount Vernon Ladies' Association, which maintains it today, is due the credit for saving Washington's home.

This organization has refurnished the house with period pieces; but year after year, through bequest, purchase and donation, the furnishings that were at Mount Vernon in the time of Washington are being acquired.

The reds and oranges of the draperies and bed hangings in the downstairs bedroom contrast with the walls.

*Above:* On December 14, 1799, General Washington died in this unadorned
canopy bed which he had ordered made in Philadelphia. *Below:* It was in the library
that Washington wrote his many letters which were so influential
in the movement for establishing a Federal Government.

*Opposite:* Monticello represents the distillation of all Jefferson's studies and exposure to fine architecture.
*Above:* The statesman died in this room on July 4, 1826. (Jefferson Memorial Foundation Photos)

# MONTICELLO
## *Jefferson's Graceful Mansion*

Monticello in Charlottesville, Virginia, is like no other home in America, so well does it express the character of its designer and builder. Thomas Jefferson was one of the first great American architects and he exercised a great influence on the designs for public and private buildings in the Classical Revival style. The great statesman candidly admitted "architecture is my delight, and putting up and pulling down, one of my favorite amusements." From early manhood until his death at eighty-three, Jefferson was engaged in building and improving Monticello.

Although a three-story building, Monticello was designed to appear as a one-story structure. There are thirty-five rooms including twelve in the basement. The dominating feature is the dome which commands the garden or west front. The dome was the first erected over an American house. The room under the

dome, octagonal in shape, is often referred to as the ballroom; however, Jefferson always referred to it as the sky or dome room.

Though the house and grounds were sold for financial reasons shortly after Jefferson's death on July 4, 1826, Monticello can be seen today much as it was when Jefferson retired to enjoy the last years of his life there among his family and his gardens. In 1923 the house and about 683 acres were purchased by the Thomas Jefferson Memorial Foundation whose purpose is to preserve the house and restore the gardens as they were in Jefferson's day. The gardens on the east and west lawns of Monticello, neglected for many years, were restored in 1939-40.

Jefferson also designed the buildings at the University of Virginia in Charlottesville, often called the most beautiful campus in the country.

The Custis-Lee Mansion in Arlington, Virginia, is distinctive
through its long association with families of historical prominence. (Anderson Photo, FPG)

# CUSTIS-LEE MANSION
## *Home of the Confederacy's General*

An 1829 graduate of West Point, Robert E. Lee married Mary Ann Randolph Custis, foster great-granddaughter of George Washington, and the Greek Revival mansion which her father had built at Arlington, Virginia, between 1802 and 1817 became their home until the outbreak of the Civil War.

With the inauguration of President Lincoln in 1861, South Carolina ratified the Ordinance of Secession and withdrew from the Union. Apprehensive of what would follow, Lee declined the request to take command of the Union Army, explaining that "though opposed to secession and deprecating war, I could take no part in an invasion of the Southern states." When Virginia ratified the secession ordinance, Lee resigned his commission and returned to Virginia, declaring that "save in defense of my native state, I never desire to draw my sword again."

Lee did draw his sword again, in defense of Virginia and the entire South, as he assumed command of the Army of the Confederacy. For nearly three years he outmaneuvered and outfought the superior forces of the Union; but when an obscure Union officer from Illinois took a determined hold on the Western extension of Lee's army and moved diligently eastward, consuming the Confederate forces on every ground, Lee's fate was sealed. On April 9, 1865, he surrendered to the commander of the Union Army, General Ulysses S. Grant.

Lee never returned to Arlington after his departure in 1861. The Union army established a garrison there from which to defend Washington and, in 1864, the estate was seized for a national cemetery.

The Custis-Lee Mansion looks out over Arlington National Cemetery, reflecting the changing architectural, as well as political, influences. A classic among the Greek Revival designs popular through the Atlantic seaboard and Southern states before the Civil War, the Custis-Lee Mansion is comprised of a large central unit, adjoined by two opposing and smaller wings. The pitched roof of the building's main element is dominated by a graceful pediment and supporting Doric columns which stand at the top of expansive, temple-like stairs. Built almost entirely of brick, all exterior walls were covered with heavy, protective plaster and deeply scored to give the impression of cut stone.

White House of the Confederacy. (Courtesy Confederate Museum Photo)

# WHITE HOUSE OF THE CONFEDERACY
## A Rebellious Nation's Executive Mansion

An angular white-stuccoed brick house at 12th and Clay streets in Richmond, Virginia, now known as the Museum of the Confederacy, was the home of Jefferson Davis and his family during the years he served as President of the Confederacy and was the South's "White House."

The house, designed by Robert Mills, was begun by Dr. John Brockenbrough in 1818. At that time it was just two stories high; the front and rear porches were adorned with Ionic and Doric columns, respectively, and a parapet encompassed the extensive flat roof. During the mid-1850's, however, the building was "Victorianized." A third story was added, above

which a small louvered cupola was installed, and the parapet around the front portion of the house was eliminated.

After the fall of Richmond, troops of the Union armies occupied the house for five years. Then for twenty years the mansion served as a schoolhouse before it was acquired by the Confederate Memorial Literary Society, which has restored several of the rooms so that they appear as they might have during the occupancy of the Davises. Among their personal possessions are a pair of Dresden vases, glass wine cooler and some decanters, and a berry bowl and silver egg boiler. Since 1893 it has also been a museum.

*Left:* A large two-story portico on the garden side of the mansion provides a cool place to sit or walk on summer evenings. *Below:* The mantel in the parlor is Carrara marble. (Keller Color Photos, courtesy Confederate Museum)

# BERKELEY
## *Homestead of the Harrisons*

Berkeley is a plantation that is by origin, incident and association as well as architecture, the stuff of history. The beautifully balanced brick mansion was built by Benjamin Harrison IV in 1726 on a slight elevation nearly a quarter of a mile back from the river. The house was made with three-foot-thick walls, hand-hewn heart pine floors and a full brick basement to serve as a wine cellar.

Two and a half stories high, Berkeley's pediment roof, said to be Virginia's first, was a significant utilitarian advance over the hip type because it provided useful end rooms in the attic without dormers (although Berkeley has three dormers on each of the fronts) and ventilation where it was needed.

Benjamin Harrison V, who signed the Declaration of Independence, had the honor of reading its preamble before Congress. His son William was the ninth President of the United States. William Henry Harrison wrote his inaugural address at Berkeley in the room where he was born. His grandson was Benjamin Harrison, the twenty-third President of the United States.

During the Civil War, Berkeley became a camping ground for General McClellan and over 100,000 Union troops, after they withdrew from Malvern Hill. It was during this period in 1862 that General Daniel Butterfield composed the world-famous bugle call, "Taps."

*Above:* Berkeley's pediment-roofed mansion has presided over the plantation since 1726. (Courtesy, Va. State Chamber of Commerce Photo.) *Opposite:* Mottled-gray marble facing of fireplace remains from early times in south end of Great Room. (Walter Miller Photo) See also page 1.

# ROLFE-WARREN HOUSE
## The Historic
## "Fifty-foot Brick House"

*Ætatis suæ 21. Aº. 1616.*

Matoaks als Rebecka daughter to the mighty Prince Powhatan Emperour of Attanoughkomouck als Virginia converted and baptized in the Christian faith, and Wife to the wor.<sup>ll</sup> M.<sup>r</sup> Tho: Rolff.

Pocahontas, wife of John Rolfe, is a colorful, legendary figure of America's past. (Courtesy National Portrait Gallery, Smithsonian Institution)

*Opposite:* This quaint colonial brick home, designed after an English country manor, was built in 1652. The land was originally presented to John Rolfe and his bride, the Indian princess Pocahontas, by her father Chief Powhatan. (Photo, courtesy The Association for the Preservation of Virginia Antiquities)

Across the James River from Jamestown, Virginia, near a high bluff, stands one of the oldest houses in America, a house built on land associated with the renowned Indian princess, Pocahontas, who married the early English colonist, John Rolfe. This "Fifty-foot Brick House," as it was known in colonial records, was erected in 1652 on a tract owned by Thomas Rolfe, only child and son of the first chief, Powhatan. Now known as the Rolfe-Warren House, the historic brick dwelling is maintained as a public museum by the Thomas Rolfe Branch of the Association for the Preservation of Virginia Antiquities.

Located in what is now Surry County, the tract was sold in 1652 by Thomas Rolfe to Thomas Warren, a burgess representing Surry in the colonial legislature. Although it is not known definitely whether Rolfe or Warren built the Fifty-foot Brick House now standing on the site, it has been determined that the dwelling was erected in 1652 and that, according to old Surry County records, Thomas Rolfe was commonly on the property "before & after & whilst ye said house was building."

Thomas Warren retained ownership of the place until his death in 1669. The several successive owners included, it is said, a "penurious farmer" in the mid-1880's who sold souvenir bricks from the house to tourists.

The historic dwelling at Smith's Fort Plantation would have fallen into complete decay had it not been for the generosity of John D. Rockefeller, Jr., who, in 1928, purchased the house and presented it to the Association for the Preservation of Virginia Antiquities. At that time, when Mr. Rockefeller was also engaged in restoring nearby Colonial Williamsburg,

he stipulated that the association restore and refurnish the house as a public museum.

It was two Colonial Williamsburg architects, Singleton P. Morehead and A. Edwin Kendrew who, in 1934, undertook the task of returning the Rolfe-Warren House as nearly as possible to its original condition. They observed that "the appearance before restoration was that of a house on the verge of ruin." They also discovered, however, that the interior woodwork was largely intact.

In reference to its design, the house has been justly acclaimed as a masterpiece of early colonial architecture — symmetrical, well balanced, harmonious and without undue ornamentation. It is said to have been modeled after an English gentleman's country seat. Resting on a high basement of English bond brickwork, the house's main portion is of ruddy brick laid in Flemish bond. It is one and one-half stories high with a steeply pitched roof containing three narrow dormers. A modest porch leads into the building's central entrance hall.

*Above:* Tryon Palace was described as the continent's finest government house when completed in 1770. *Opposite:* The lavish State Dining Room includes a Turkish carpet. (Courtesy Tryon Palace Photos)

# TRYON PALACE
## *Monument to a Governor's Vanity*

North Carolina's colonial governor had grandiose visions for his province-house built in New Bern. Governor William Tryon was charged with "gratifying his vanity," with building an "elegant monument of his taste and political influence at the expense of the interest of the province, and of his personal honor." The architecture of Tryon Palace, described as "the most beautiful building in the colonial Americas," was unique in the New World in that it was designed as a London vicinity house, and served not only as the colonial capitol but also as the governor's residence. Construction of the original large edifice and its two wings was begun in 1767 and finished in 1770 under the supervision of John Hawks, English master builder and "the first professional architect to remain in America."

The main building was destroyed by fire in 1798. Through trusts and bequests of the late Mrs. James Edwin Latham, a native of New Bern, the restoration of the palace on Pollock Street was begun in 1952 and completed in 1959. Extensive research has been put into the accurate redecoration of the palace. Furnished throughout with genuine eighteenth-century antiques, mostly predating 1770, the restored palace is almost a shrine for connoisseurs of early furniture, housewares, paintings, printed material, textiles, carpets and the accessories of twenty-seven large fireplaces.

*Left:* The Royal Coat of Arms of King George III appears at the front of Tryon Palace. Made of carved and emblazoned mahogany, the escutcheon of the House of Hanover is the central feature. The two mottos read, "Shame be to him who evil thinks" and "God and my right."

*Above:* Delicate wrought-iron gates and railing mark the approach to the Tryon Palace in New Bern, North Carolina. The unique English-style home, begun in 1767, became the first fixed colonial capitol of the state in 1770 and also served as the governor's residence.

Audubon House was built in the Bahama style with wooden pegs rather than nails. (Courtesy Wometco Enterprises, Inc. Photos)

# AUDUBON HOUSE
## An Eclectic Gulf Coast Dwelling

From the windows of this white frame structure, two men could, indeed did, look out toward the Gulf of Mexico in the year 1832 and find entirely different things of absorbing interest. To Captain John H. Geiger who built this house two years earlier, the sight of a floundering ship may not have sparked surprise, but it did move him to action. Salvage was his business — a profitable one, too, in that period when Key West, Florida, was a graveyard of pirated ships.

But to John James Audubon, the naturalist and painter, the exotic flowers and birds of rare plumage were visions unmatched by any encountered in his previous travels. From the Geiger house where Audubon remained a guest throughout that year, he painted a pair of white-crowned pigeons in the Geiger tree. This painting and another — of the Key West Pigeon, identified in his "elephant" or double folio edition of 435 watercolors of birds as the Key West Quail

Dove — were among those completed during his stay. The folio was published by Robert Havell & Son in London in four volumes entitled *Birds of America*. It appeared between 1827 and 1839, cost $1,000 then (about $30,000 now) and was one of the largest books ever printed.

It was the association of these two men that determined the manner and style in which the Geiger House, now called Audubon House, would be restored by the Mitchell Wolfson Foundation in 1960. Constructed in the so-called Bahama style — all timbers were joined by wooden pegs and not a nail was used in its construction — the house also stands as a reminder of the period when there was still local fear of Indian attacks. In spite of Captain Geiger's status as a wealthy, highly respected member of the community, his house was built on a small plot of land close to other dwellings for protection from Indian forays.

# THE HERMITAGE
*Andrew Jackson's Pillared Mansion*

*Above:* The front portico of The Hermitage is supported by six fluted columns with cast-iron capitals.
*Opposite:* The hall wallpaper depicts Greek legends. (Courtesy Ladies' Hermitage Association Photos)

The Hermitage near Donelson, Tennessee, was the home of Andrew Jackson, seventh President of the United States, hero of the Battle of New Orleans and Tennessee's greatest and most renowned son.

Andrew Jackson was a national figure, generally recognized as one of the nation's greatest Presidents. He was of Scots-Irish descent, born March 15, 1767, in Lancaster County, South Carolina, the son of Andrew and Elizabeth Hutchinson Jackson of Carrickfergus, Ireland.

Jackson's father died before he was born. The extent of his formal education is not known, but as a young man, Jackson was a hard worker, aggressive and a fine judge of horseflesh. He studied law and applied himself so earnestly that by the time he was twenty he was licensed to practice law.

Jackson's marriage to Rachel Donelson Robards was one of considerable controversy. They were married in 1791 and not until two years later, in the fall of 1793, did they learn that Rachel had never been legally divorced from her first husband, Captain Lewis Robards. At first Jackson opposed a second wedding, but in January 1794, they were married a second time.

Jackson's achievements as a military commander won him national recognition and put him on the road to the White House. He emerged from the War of 1812 as the most able field commander in the country and earned the nickname, "Old Hickory," for his firm resolution and daring.

The original Hermitage was built in 1819 and was a brick structure, probably designed by Jackson himself. In this unpretentious home Jackson and his wife lived for nine years until Rachel's death. In 1831, while Jackson was President, the Hermitage was extensively remodeled and improved, but in 1834, the roof of the Hermitage caught fire and much of the building was lost. Although a financial blow to him, Jackson had the home rebuilt.

Jackson died in 1845. The Hermitage and its 625 acres is now maintained by the Ladies Hermitage Association, organized in 1889 to preserve the estate. Outstanding about the Hermitage, aside from its stately appearance and manicured, British-designed garden, is that it is the only national shrine furnished completely with original pieces.

# WILLIAM FAULKNER HOME
## *Rowan Oak*

There is an old Welsh legend of which William Faulkner was particularly fond which claimed that, wherever it grew, the Rowan oak tree would keep away all evil. When he and his wife bought a house situated deep in a woodland of magnificent oak trees they named the place Rowan Oak.

William Faulkner lived and worked at Rowan Oak, Oxford, Mississippi, from 1930 until his death in 1962 and produced the major portion of his work here.

Rowan Oak, intact since 1840, was built by Robert Shegog, a trader, who was among the first pioneers to settle in the Chickasaw country. Originally a primitive farmhouse, the Faulkners made improvements and additions while taking great care to retain the original architectural lines.

Directly opposite the library is the sanctum sanctorum of Rowan Oak. This was Faulkner's office, a place exclusively his own where horse liniment and tobacco pouch could be placed side by side without ever being disturbed. In this office, along with the many personal effects, Faulkner left what many distinguished scholars call the most famous literary wall in the world. On it is the complex outline of his book, *A Fable*, which is an allegorical novel about mutiny in the front lines during World War I.

Nobel Prize-winner William Faulkner did much writing at Rowan Oak. (University of Mississippi Library Photo)

Grouseland was said to be the finest brick mansion in Vincennes. (CB Photos)

# GROUSELAND
## *William Henry Harrison's Mansion*

When William Henry Harrison built the house he called Grouseland in 1804, he was Governor of the Indiana Territory, a land mass larger than that occupied by all the states at that time. Initially this territory included only the present states of Indiana, Illinois, Michigan, Wisconsin and eastern Minnesota; but with the Louisiana Purchase of 1803, its boundaries were expanded to include Missouri, Arkansas, Iowa, western Minnesota, Kansas, Nebraska, Colorado, North Dakota, South Dakota, Montana, Wyoming and Oklahoma. Although this expansive domain was short-lived as the Indiana Territory, Grouseland, from which Harrison ministered his official duties, became known as the "White House of the West."

Located along the upper reaches of the Wabash River at Vincennes, Indiana, Grouseland was constructed in a walnut grove after the Georgian style of tidewater Virginia. It is a spacious, two-story brick structure with false windows, secret passages and the legend of a tunnel somewhere on the grounds, even though there is no evidence to support this assertion.

It was built during a time of upheaval among the Indians, and is noted for having been the site where five treaties were signed with northern tribes. Among the many distinguished visitors to Grouseland were the Indian Chief Tecumseh and his brother the Prophet, who came to utter their dissatisfaction over the cession of Indian lands.

Standing in the midst of the walnut grove before the mansion, Tecumseh is reputed to have charged: "Sell a country! Why not sell the air, the clouds and the great sea, as well as the earth? Did not the great spirit make them all for the use of his children?"

Discouraged with the endless treaties, Tecumseh did not return to Grouseland after 1811. In the fall of that year Harrison met and defeated Tecumseh at Tippecanoe Creek. Harrison's campaign slogan, "Tippecanoe and Tyler too," in his Presidential election victory of 1840 was a reference to that battle. A more important battlefield triumph for Harrison, however, took place in October 1813, near the Thames River in Canada, north of Lake Erie. This time Tecumseh was slain and troops lead by Harrison captured an entire British force. As a result, the United States was in undisputed possession of the Great Lakes except for Lake Ontario.

69

*Above:* The graceful stairway, similar to those found in Virginia, has cherry treads, risers and banister.
*Opposite:* In the parlor, the portrait of the serious, quizzical young Harrison in dress uniform is by Rembrandt Peale.

In 1812 Harrison had moved his family back to his country home in North Bend, Ohio, and he resigned as governor. After the conclusion of the war in 1814, he resigned his command and returned to Ohio. Harrison remained there until he achieved the Presidency in 1840, when he defeated Martin Van Buren.

For a period of about four or five years after the war, the house at Grouseland was occupied by Judge Benjamin Parke, reverting back to the Harrison family in 1819 when Harrison's son, John Cleves Symmes Harrison, settled there with his family. In 1850 the house passed out of the family for the last time, and was used as a hotel and a granary until 1860, when it again became a residence.

In 1909 the Vincennes Water Company bought the house and was about to destroy it when the Francis Vigo Chapter of the Daughters of the American Revolution intervened. Raising funds to preserve the house, the D.A.R. opened it to the public in 1910, and in 1949 some restoration work was done. It wasn't until 1963, however, that extensive restoration was begun.

# ULYSSES S. GRANT HOUSE
*Sam Grant's Galena Mansion*

In 1865 Ulysses S. Grant was presented this handsome two-story brick residence in Galena, Illinois, by private citizens as a tribute to the victorious general.

Ulysses S. Grant arrived in Galena in the spring of 1860 by steamboat to clerk in the family leather goods store, and five years later the town was to present the victorious Union general with one of the finest Victorian homes in the city during a grand victory celebration.

The house on Bouthillier Street, not far from the Galena River, was built in 1859. Designed in the Italianate bracketed style, the two-story brick residence with wide, overhanging eaves, represented the best mid-Victorian architecture of the period.

Although Grant always considered the Galena home his legal residence, the period after the war until his death in 1885, including his terms as President during 1869-77, allowed him little time there. The mansion remained in the family until 1904 when it was deeded to Galena.

In 1932 the house passed to the State of Illinois and, in 1955, a complete restoration was undertaken. Use of the original plans and specifications, drawn by the builder in 1859, permitted authentic structural restoration and many of the original Grant furnishings were available for the interior. Among these, an old horsehair-covered parlor set is displayed on a new loop Brussels carpet, containing the same colors and exact pattern as the original. The Haviland china displayed in the dining room was bought for Grant's daughter in 1874.

Handsome set on the dining room table is Haviland china bought in 1874. (Illinois Dept. of Conservation Photo)

*Above:* Native hardwoods, white pine and hand-split hickory laths went into the Springfield home Lincoln bought in 1844. *Opposite:* Globes flank the red-patterned sofa near fireplace. (CB Photos)

# ABRAHAM LINCOLN HOME
## *Lincoln's Springfield Years*

By 1844, Abraham Lincoln was rapidly approaching political prominence. He had already served four terms in the Illinois State Legislature, participated in two law firms as a junior partner and played an active role in the Presidential campaign of 1840, which brought the Whigs their first victory in the person of William Henry Harrison.

It was in this year that Lincoln bought a one-and-a-half-story cottage in Springfield, Illinois, for $1,500 from the Reverend Charles Dresser, who had married him to Mary Todd two years earlier. Except for one year (1847) during his term in the United States Congress, Lincoln occupied this house until he left Springfield as President-elect in 1861.

Three of Lincoln's sons were born in this house and one died there. The death of Edward Baker Lincoln in 1850 at the age of four foreshadowed future tragedies that would weigh on the Lincoln family during the Presidential years.

Built in 1839, the two-story frame house, which has been preserved on the original Eighth and Jackson Streets' site, achieved its final form when Mary Todd Lincoln added the extra half-story in 1856. Reflected in its delicate trim and cornices, the house was designed in the Greek Revival style as it appeared on the frontier, framed in oak and sided and floored with black walnut.

Architecturally, it is a modest representative of the pre-Civil War era. What is most meaningful about it is that the purchase of this home marked the division between Lincoln's interest in local and state politics and his embarkation into national affairs. At this time he was on the verge of gaining a seat in the U.S. Congress after two previous and unsuccessful attempts.

The piano was played at Lincoln's wedding in 1842. Other possessions are on view in the well-restored sitting room.

In 1846 Lincoln was elected to the U.S. Congress. This was a disheartening period for both Lincoln and his constituents, however, and at the end of the term, Lincoln himself confessed that he would not be able to muster enough support to seek the office a second time. His only notable accomplishment during these two years was an unpopular stand against President Polk's promotion of the Mexican War. Persistently, he demanded that the President prove the war was not a product of United States' aggression.

Even before this debacle in Congress, after which he returned indefinitely to his law practice, there were forces at work throughout the country which would preclude his retirement from politics for very

long. There was great sectional turmoil over the extension of slavery into the Western territories, and as early as 1837, Lincoln had expressed a strong moral objection to that institution.

In 1858 Senator Douglas was up for re-election. Through his opposition to the Kansas-Nebraska Act and vigorous support of Frémont, Lincoln won the opportunity to oppose Douglas. In the months prior to the election, Lincoln challenged Douglas to a series of public debates which inevitably focused on the slavery issue. In continuous attacks against the Southern slaveholders and Northern liberals, Lincoln told the nation, "Familiarize yourselves with the chains of bondage and you are preparing yourselves to wear them. ...You have lost the genius of your own independence and become fit subjects for the first cunning tyrant who rises among you."

Lincoln lost the election, but he gained politically. With the approach of the 1860 Presidential election, Lincoln was so closely identified with the slavery issue that he was the natural champion of the Republican cause. Numerical superiority of the free states over the slave states, by this time, assured Lincoln of a majority in a wide field of candidates; and in 1861, as President-elect, he left Illinois forever. Speaking almost prophetically to a group of friends who accompanied him to the railroad station, he said: "Here I have lived for a quarter of a century .... Here my children have been born and one is buried .... I now leave, not knowing when, or whether ever, I may return .... "

Today Lincoln's Springfield house, maintained as a memorial by the State of Illinois, contains some of the original furnishings: Lincoln's hatrack in the downstairs hallway; the dining room has the Lincolns' dessert service on the card table; the reproduced Brussels carpet and horsehair sofa are in the living room; Lincoln's favorite horsehair-covered rocker is in the sitting room; his secretary is in the back parlor; and his shaving mirror and chest of drawers are in his bedroom.

Hanging above Robert Lincoln's spool bed is an embroidered Old Glory, crafted when Wisconsin entered the Union.

# HULL HOUSE
## *Jane Addams in Chicago*

Jane Addams grew to maturity during the last years of the nineteenth century, when the rapid expansion of industry and transportation and a great influx in immigration produced severe slum conditions in most urban areas throughout the country. She was to become a potent force in combating those conditions and alleviating their unfortunate results.

During a restless and unhappy period after her father's death, she traveled twice to Europe and these journeys seemed to help her to find the purpose in life that she was seeking. She became acutely aware of the poverty in Europe, and in Madrid, during the second trip (1887-1888), her ideas seemed to crystallize. She decided to open a settlement house for the underprivileged.

Before returning to America, she visited Toynbee Hall, an English settlement house, the first in the world, established to ease slum conditions there. Back in this country, she went to Chicago to begin her project, settling on the Charles J. Hull mansion as her headquarters several months later.

An adaption of Greek Revival design, the two-story mansion, built in 1856, had a large portico which extended around three sides and was supported by tall Corinthian columns.

The purpose of Hull House was to stimulate social and cultural growth as well as to feed, clothe and help find jobs for the thousands of immigrant families. A kindergarten for the children of working mothers and an employment bureau were followed later by an art gallery, library and a music and crafts school. By the turn of the century, twelve additional buildings were incorporated into Hull House, including a theater, gymnasium, nursery, residents' dining hall and apartments for residents.

The heterogeneous population that surrounded Hull House emphasized the need for different nationalities to live peacefully together. Applying this concept to national affairs, Jane Addams joined the Women's Peace Party. For her subsequent organization and leadership of the International Women's League for Peace and Freedom, in 1931 Jane Addams became the first American woman to receive the Nobel Peace Prize.

Jane Addams used the Hull mansion for the first settlement house in this country. (University of Illinois Photo)

Years after the adventures which produced the characters of Tom Sawyer and Huckleberry Finn, Mark Twain returned to Hannibal, Missouri.

# MARK TWAIN HOME
## *Hannibal: Home of an American Original*

The Mark Twain Home in Hannibal is known throughout the world as the Mississippi River home of Tom Sawyer in the fictional town of St. Petersburg. It was here that Mark Twain (Samuel Langhorne Clemens) was raised and experienced many of the adventures which later produced the tales of Tom Sawyer and Huckleberry Finn.

The two-story frame house was built in 1844 by John Marshall Clemens, Sam's father. George A. Mahan, an avid Mark Twain admirer, purchased it in 1912. Presenting the home intact to the town of Hannibal, and later contributing bronze statues of both Tom Sawyer and Hucklberry Finn, Mahan established the first of many memorials to Twain.

With the interior restored to its nineteenth century appearance, the house at 206 Hill Street is again the scene where young Sam Clemens administered pain killer to Peter the cat and escaped out of a second-story window to meet Tom Blankenship (later known as Huckleberry Finn) for a round of midnight pranks. Here, also, his mother, his sister Pamela and brother Henry were later transformed into the characters of Aunt Polly, Mary and Sid. The original board fence around the house which Clemens, and later Tom Sawyer, duped neighborhood boys into whitewashing for him is gone, but a duplicate now stands in its place.

# ALEXANDER RAMSEY HOUSE
*The Governor's Ornate Victorian Residence*

*Above:* Three generations of the Ramsey family lived in the Walnut Street mansion. *Opposite:* Flanking the reception room fireplace are a pair of sleepy hollow chairs. (Minnesota Historical Society Photos)

The "Mansion House marking the full accomplishment of a Pennsylvania Dutch burgher" named Alexander Ramsey, is also a monument to the remarkable transformation of Minnesota in the middle of the nineteenth century. In treaties made in 1837, the Chippewa and the Sioux Indians relinquished title to the valued wedge of land·between the Mississippi and St. Croix rivers. Twelve years later Congress passed a bill organizing the Territory of Minnesota, and on May 27, 1849, Ramsey, its first territorial governor, arrived by steamboat in St. Paul, at the capital — "just emerging from a collection of Indian whiskey shops and birch-roofed cabins of half-breed voyageurs." The population of the territory would grow from 300 to 150,037 in a brief eight years.

It was not sheer wanderlust but diligent and clever politics that propelled Ramsey west. "A hearty, heavy, hard-fisted" man, Ramsey "wasted no time on fanciful projects," was elected mayor of St. Paul in 1855 and was chosen second governor of the newly formed State of Minnesota in 1859. Before his second term ended, he was elected United States Senator, an office he held for twelve years. He continued his public service as Secretary of War in the cabinet of President Rutherford B. Hayes.

Ramsey and his family lived in a neat "white frame cottage," actually made of logs covered with board siding, then in a "handsome, spacious house," which was in turn moved from his Walnut Street property to make way in 1872 for the gray limestone "Mansion House" in St. Paul. Ramsey's newest house, dominating the city's most prosperous and stylish neighborhood and developed from "oak scrub and swamp," was the work of many hands, talents and influences. It took the architect Monroe Scheire, the contractor John Summers and a chief carpenter, Matthew Taylor, to build the ornate three-story house with full basement, attic and mansard roof that was to serve the Ramsey family for three generations. The style of the architecture has been called, rather grandly, French Renaissance, but gentle Victorian seems more appropriate.

The mansion that was hailed by the *St. Paul Daily Press* as the "new and elegant residence," was willed to the Minnesota Historical Society in 1964 by Alexander Ramsey's grandchildren and is now in the last phase of a major restoration project.

A two-room cottage in West Branch, Iowa, was the birthplace of Herbert Hoover. (Phil McCafferty Photo)

# HERBERT HOOVER BIRTHPLACE COTTAGE
## *A President's Iowa Boyhood*

The dedication of the Herbert Hoover Presidential Library at his birthplace in August 1962, provided a permanent testimony to his own belief: "Many of the great leaders were, it is true, of humble origin, but that alone was not their greatness."

The two-room cottage in West Branch, Iowa — on which restoration work was begun in 1938 and opened to visitors the following year — was built around 1870 by Hoover's father, Jesse Clark Hoover, a Quaker blacksmith. Here, four years later, "Bert," as he was affectionately nicknamed, was born the second of three children and spent his first years.

At seventeen, Hoover left for Palo Alto, California, where he received a Bachelor of Arts degree in geology with the first graduating class at Stanford University in 1895.

He circled the globe five times before World War I, one of his more exciting experiences taking place around the turn of the century.

Altogether, Hoover served in the cabinets or headed commissions of five Presidents, serving four years in the Presidency himself. During his single term in office, his administration was responsible for, among other things, reforms of the criminal procedure for Federal courts and organization of the Federal Bureau of Investigation as an effective agency. With the crash of the stock market in October 1929, however, the country was immersed in panic. Despite Hoover's unprecedented attempts to stabilize the national economy, the fear and uncertainty which prevailed in almost all quarters of American life signaled the end of his political career.

The house belongs to the Eisenhower Museum, dedicated to servicemen and women of World War II.

# EISENHOWER FAMILY HOME
## *The General From Abilene*

The boyhood home of General and former President Dwight David Eisenhower — now part of the Eisenhower Center at Abilene, Kansas — is a memorial to Eisenhower, and to the simple and vigorous family which produced this successful soldier and statesman. It was built in the 1880's by Eisenhower's grandfather, the Reverend Jacob Eisenhower, and is typical of the two-story, frame houses which were common throughout the Midwest at the time.

Eisenhower's decision to attend a service academy after he left high school was partially derived from an earlier interest in military history.

The years between his admission to West Point and the end of World War II brought Eisenhower to one of the heights of his military career and to the brink of political prominence, as well. Returning as a great world hero to his Abilene home from Europe in 1945, Eisenhower was greeted by his aging mother the year before her death. His father had died three years earlier. In 1947 the five surviving Eisenhower brothers, Arthur, Edgar, Dwight, Earl and Milton donated the house to the Eisenhower Foundation in Abilene, which has since given it to the United States as a shrine to all the men and women who served in the armed forces during World War II.

# FAIRVIEW
*William Jennings Bryan's "Feudal Castle"*

*Opposite:* A visitor to massive Fairview said the house breathed an air of "open-handed hospitality." (Courtesy Nebraska State Hist. Soc.) *Right:* The entrance hall is hung with a portrait of a determined-looking Bryan. (CB Photo)

William Jennings Bryan, the Great Commoner, had a bond with the average person that had nothing to do with political philosophy and everything to do with private budgeting. He, like so many others, had spent more than he planned on his house. It was designed to "cost about $10,000 but owing to the numerous alterations in the plans, to the expense of delivering material so far from town and to the recent increased expense of building, the house cost considerably more than I anticipated it would," Jennings said of his Lincoln, Nebraska, home.

If Bryan's home was controversial, its master was provocative and perplexing. Theodore Roosevelt thought him "a personally honest and rather attractive man, a real orator and a born demagogue, who has every crank, fool and putative criminal in the country behind him, and a large proportion of the ignorant honest class." Bryan, who was the losing candidate for the President of the United States three different times, was a spellbinding orator, yet it was said that "one could drive a prairie schooner through any part of his argument and never scrape against a fact." As Secretary of State under Woodrow Wilson his convictions led him to resign when Wilson broke his policy of strict neutrality. He, of course, defended prohibition,

refused to condemn the Ku Klux Klan and was thought to have "undignified associations" with the promotion of Florida real estate. But it was during the Scopes anti-evolution trial in Dayton, Tennessee, that Bryan was so "pitilessly exposed." Bryan maintained, among other things, that Eve was actually made from Adam's rib and that Jonah had really been swallowed by the whale. It is the opinion of one historian anyway, that "it would have been better for Bryan's reputation if he had died in 1915; instead he lived on for another decade, as amiable and well-intentioned as ever but increasingly out of touch with the rapidly changing times."

The Bryans spent exactly fifteen years in the home where they had intended to spend the "remainder of our days except such time as may be devoted to travel." Mrs. Bryan's arthritic condition required a move to a warmer climate and Miami was their choice. The couple deeded Fairview and part of its acreage to the Bryan Memorial Hospital. It served as a dormitory for student nurses until 1961, and one year later members of the hospital board and the Junior League began a project of restoring the first floor and recreating the benevolent atmosphere of cluttered affluence enjoyed by Bryan and his wife.

Beside a bust of Bryan in the front parlor is an elephant table from India. (CB Photo)

A portrait of Young hangs in the entry hall with its hardwood paneling.
(Photos: courtesy Church of Jesus Christ of Latter-Day Saints)

# BEEHIVE HOUSE
## *Mansion of the Mormons' Pioneer Leader*

Beehive House in Salt Lake City, Utah, was aptly named. From the time the Mormon leader Brigham Young built the elaborate, pillared, Greek Revival mansion in 1854, it swarmed with family and followers who had labored their way west by oxen and mule-drawn covered wagons, by cart and by foot, through ominous Indian country and soaring mountains, to enter the valley of the Great Salt Lake, to colonize and literally to found the forty-fifth state of the Union. If the Mormons, more accurately known as Latter-Day Saints, had had their way, Utah would have been called Deseret which, in their own language, means a honeybee, the Mormon symbol of industry. Instead, they settled for a beehive-shaped gilded finial crowning the square cupola atop their leader's house as a symbol of their persistent belief that if they wanted to build up the Kingdom of God or establish Zion upon earth they would have to work — to heed Young's plea to "labor with our hands, plan

with our minds and devise ways and means to accomplish that object."

Young was living in Mendon, New York, when he was introduced to the teachings of Joseph Smith, the founding father of the Church of Jesus Christ of Latter-Day Saints. In 1830 Smith published the *Book of Mormon;* a few weeks later it was in Young's hands and after two years of study, Young left the Methodist Church irrevocably. At Smith's violent death, Young assumed leadership of the Mormons whose faith evoked bitter criticism from outsiders who did not share their view of right to plural marriage or polygamy as a religious principle. The Mormons, therefore, were made unwelcome in state after state — expelled from Ohio, from Missouri, from Illinois — and finally they made their way west to settle on what was then Mexican soil, beyond American jurisdiction. They were free now to follow the principles of Mormonism so ardently espoused by Young himself who had nineteen wives and fifty-six children in all.

The Territory of Utah was organized in September of 1850 and Young appointed governor by President Millard Fillmore and reappointed by President Franklin Pierce. Congress in President Lincoln's adminstration passed a law in 1862 against plural marriages and it was only when the Mormons would forsake polygamy entirely that the Territory of Utah was admitted into the Union, in January of 1896.

The history of the Church of the Latter-Day Saints during Young's thirty years of leadership is largely the history and settlement of the inter-mountain west during the same period. Young and the Mormons founded schools (the University of Utah was known originally as the University of Deseret),

built theaters, a newspaper, and created Zion's Co-operative Mercantile Institution which grew into the largest institution of its kind in the West.

It was just seven years after Young reached the Great Basin that he was able to build a handsome three-story house with the help of Truman O. Angell — its deep porches and balconies, its tall pillars echoing, in many ways, the mansions of Young's native Vermont with their high ceilings and expansive rooms. The Beehive House served as his office, as well as a dwelling for one family or another; the adjacent Lion House coped with overflow for the last twenty-three years of Young's life.

*Below:* Molded extension table on pedestal base and Victorian sideboard with spool-turned legs furnish mansion's dining room.
*Opposite:* The balconies and tall pillars of Beehive House echo the mansions of Brigham Young's native Vermont.

*Above:* Stone cutters imported from Scotland built the Bowers Mansion. (Bucket of Blood Saloon Photo, Virginia City, Nevada) *Opposite:* The choicest piece in the parlor is a tufted satin Louis XVI sofa. (CB Photo)

# BOWERS MANSION
## *Palace of the Tragic Queen of Washoe*

The story of the Bowers Mansion in Washoe County, Nevada, a fantastic tale of wealth and desperation, was narrated, years before it occurred, in the crystal ball of Allison Orrum. She was obsessed with dreams of great wealth growing out of the impoverishment of her early surroundings. Drawn by visions of Western mountains, criss-crossed by wagon tracks and laboring men, she accompanied her sister and brother-in-law to the Mormon settlement of Nauvoo, Illinois, where she observed in her crystal ball, "I'll have more money than I know what to do with, but I'll be poor again."

Her first impression of the Mormon community was disappointing, but she married one of the elders and, consulting her crystal ball frequently, she accompanied him to Brigham Young's settlement near the Great Salt Lake. But it soon became evident that her fortune did not lie in the Mormon community.

Finding a younger man whom she felt she could control, "Eilley" Bowers remarried and urged the man to take her to Washoe County, Nevada, near the Comstock. There the mines were belching forth their wealth, but her new husband wasn't interested in forcefully pursuing the fortune that was within reach. Thus when the Mormon settlement again decided to move, Eilley sent her husband along with it, ending her second marriage and she continued her quest alone.

For several months she supported herself at the site of the mines by cooking and washing for the prospectors, until one discouraged miner offered his ten-foot claim in payment of his account. Then, as rapidly as before, she married the man who operated the adjoining claim — Sandy Bowers — and secured her contract with destiny.

The fortune that followed this marriage accumulated at the rate of $18,000 per day at the height of the Comstock boom, and the mansion which was born out of the fortune reflected every extravagance

the sudden prosperity could imagine. Originally a huge two-story building surrounded by balustraded porticos on the first and second levels and capped by an adorning rail and cupola on the roof, the house was begun in 1861 and completed in 1864. Stone cutters were imported from Scotland to quarry the marble blocks from the nearby mountains, and so precisely did they work that no mortar was needed to join them. The expansive grounds were meticulously landscaped and swimming pools were constructed, filled with natural warm water from nearby springs. A fountain in front of the mansion forms a pool which was stocked with goldfish. The lavish furnishings for the house were almost without exception imported from Europe during a year-and-a-half tour, the extravagance of which reputedly overwhelmed the traditional garnishes of the *nouveaux riches*.

Toward the end of the decade, there was marked concern over production at the Comstock, and in 1868, Sandy died trying to re-establish the mine after the devastation of the previous winter. While the estate was under settlement, Eilley discovered that their fortune had been drained through the widespread speculation that now threatened the future of the entire Comstock.

In the following years, Eilley attempted to save the house by transforming it into a tourist hotel. Although undaunted by a succession of disappointments in this venture, Eilley was finally crushed by the death of her daughter in 1874. She left the mansion to wander as a clairvoyant, first through Virginia City, then finally to San Francisco where she died in 1903.

The mansion and grounds served as a beer garden through the next 40 years until it was purchased in 1946 by the Reno Women's Civic Club. Restored as authentically as possible, the house and grounds were incorporated into Washoe County as a memorial park.

Mrs. Bowers' private rooms have been restored with the original furnishings. (Bucket of Blood Saloon Photo, Virginia City, Nevada)

The primitive but cheerful kitchen has a large bell-shaped cooking fireplace built into the corner of the room. (Kit Carson Memorial Foundation Photo)

# KIT CARSON HOME
## *House of a Hero*

When Kit Carson bought this twelve-room, adobe house in Taos, New Mexico, for his Spanish bride in 1843, his reputation as an Indian fighter and frontiersman was already well established. He would become even more prominent for his exploits of heroism during the Mexican and Civil Wars, but this house would be Carson's permanent residence until he died twenty-five years later. He would be away from Taos much of the time during those years, but six and probably seven of his eight children were born there and seven of his more rewarding as well as frustrating years would be spent there as Indian agent.

Constructed in 1825 by an unidentified owner, the house is a single-story affair, designed in stockade fashion around a central patio or garden. Peculiar in its construction were the different levels of each of the rooms, caused by raising the walls of the house first and then packing the dirt floors to the easiest

accessible level in each room. Until a saw mill was available in the 1860's the dirt floors were retained throughout the house. The exterior walls of the building were constructed from adobe brick, reaching a thickness of 30 inches, and covered with an adobe plaster material. Exposed ceiling beams of peeled logs jutted through this outer wall and supported a dirt roof also several feet thick. To provide heat and cooking facilities, fireplaces were built into practically every room.

After 1868, the Carson house passed through no less than six owners when, in 1910, it was purchased and restored by the Masonic Lodge of Taos. It wasn't until 1952, however, that the Kit Carson Memorial Foundation was established and the house opened to the public. Today, three of the rooms have been restored, using many of the original furnishings, to reflect a living room, kitchen and bedroom of the Carson era.

# LELAND STANFORD HOUSE
*A Keepsake of a Tycoon*

Gold was not the only source of fortune-making in California in the middle of the nineteenth century: Railroad construction was definitely another way up the financial ladder; and one man who successfully climbed it was Leland Stanford. Stanford, an Easterner and a lawyer who was far from the run-of-the-mill pioneer, arrived in California in 1852, just two years after the state's admission to the Union. During his lifetime, Stanford served as governor of his state and as senator, and left an enduring monument in the form of the superb educational institution, Stanford University, named after his son who died of typhoid fever at the age of fifteen.

It was inevitable that a man with Leland Stanford's vision would have the desire and the need for a splendid setting for his increasingly affluent life and social responsibilities. Stanford bought the perfect house in Sacramento in 1861. It had been built for Shelton C. Fogus, a Virginian who had gone off to fortune hunt in Nevada and to help found Reno. Stanford's new home was the work of Seth Babson, an emigré from Maine, who had been commissioned to design a "fine house of brick and plaster." It turned out to be that and much more, a marvelous Victorian concoction of French and Italian inclinations, "finished in a costly manner."

Stanford was elected Governor of California the year after his purchase and he is supposed to have rowed home from his inaugural ceremony due to a flood that submerged his house in water up to its parlor windows. About three hundred wagon loads of silt and debris later, and the planting of seven or eight hundred trees, plants and vines afterwards, Stanford's house was once more in order and ready for some extraordinary expansion: The first floor was raised one story, and a stairway and porch were added to maintain the same entrance.

The Stanfords left Sacramento for San Francisco in 1874 and seven years after his husband's death in 1893, Mrs. Jane Lathrop Stanford deeded the Sacramento home to the Catholic Diocese of Sacramento. The adolescent girls who live there now are enveloped in the pageantry of the nineteenth-century interior, its furniture a keepsake of the extravagant past.

*Opposite and above:* A gracefully arching double staircase of white-painted wood rises to a porch with Corinthian columns. The porch protects tall carved mahogany doors with their superb etched and cut glass. *Below:* Dominating the entrance hall is a massive Eastlake-style hat and umbrella stand complete with fluted columns. (B.B.M. Associates Photos)

Franciscan missionary Junipero Serra died here. (John M. Nuhn)

# SAN CARLOS BORROMEO DEL RIO CARMELO MISSION
## *Junipero Serra's Headquarters*

In the late eighteenth century, the coast of California was the scene of much missionary activity. Foremost among the Franciscan missionaries was Junipero Serra, who walked thousands of miles in his lifetime in pursuit of his noble calling. In addition to his proselytizing the Indians, he also built missions and facilitated the settling of the area.

Spanish-born Father Serra did not surround himself with luxury in his headquarters at the San Carlos Borromeo mission near Carmel. His tiny cell near the church held a cot of boards, a single blanket, a table and chair, a chest, a candlestick and a gourd.

The rough-hewn beauty of San Carlos Borromeo del Rio Carmelo makes her the romantic jewel of the California chain of missions. Set in the lovely Carmel area of the Monterey Peninsula, this mission was Father Junipero Serra's favorite and his headquarters for the entire California chain of twenty-one missions

stretching 700 miles, from San Diego to Sonoma, along *El Camino Real,* California's first road.

Only the second mission to be founded, in 1771, the present stone edifice was not dedicated until 1797, thirteen years after Father Serra's death. He is buried beneath the church.

This is a solidly built church, designed by a master craftsman and fashioned by devoted Indian pupils. Rough sandstone walls and intriguing unequal Moorish towers are highlighted by the striking star window "that seems to have been blown out of shape in some wintery wind, and all its lines hardened again in the sunshine of the long, long summer."

The mission was secularized in 1834 and for many years was left in neglect. Complete restoration was begun in the 1930's. Extensive research has been done into physical and written church records, resulting in an extremely authentic restoration.

96